Living With Xenophobia: Zimbabwean Informal Enterprise in South Africa

Jonathan Crush, Godfrey Tawodzera, Abel Chikanda
and Daniel Tevera

SAMP MIGRATION POLICY SERIES NO. 77

Series Editor: Prof. Jonathan Crush

Southern African Migration Programme (SAMP)
2017

AUTHORS

Jonathan Crush is the CIGI Chair in Global Migration and Development at the Balsillie School of International Affairs, Waterloo, Canada.

Godfrey Tawodzera is a Senior Lecturer in the Department of Geography and Environmental Studies, University of Limpopo, Polokwane, South Africa.

Abel Chikanda is Assistant Professor of Geography and African & African American Studies at the University of Kansas, Lawrence, Kansas, United States.

Daniel Tevera is a Professor in the Department of Geography, Environmental Studies and Tourism at the University of the Western Cape, South Africa.

ACKNOWLEDGEMENTS

We would like to acknowledge the support of the IDRC-funded Growing Informal Cities (GIC) Project and the Migrants in Countries in Crisis (MICIC) Initiative of the International Migration Policy Development Centre (IMPDC) and the International Migration Institute (IMI) at Oxford University.

© Southern African Migration Programme (SAMP) 2017

Published by the Southern African Migration Programme, International Migration Research Centre, Balsillie School of International Affairs, Waterloo, Ontario, Canada samponline.org

First published 2017

ISBN 978-1-920596-37-8

Cover photo by James Oatway

Production by Bronwen Dachs Muller, Cape Town

Printed by The Printing Press, Cape Town

CONTENTS

PAGE

LIST OF TABLES

LIST OF FIGURES

EXECUTIVE SUMMARY

South Africa's crisis of xenophobia is defined by the discrimination and intolerance to which migrants are exposed on a daily basis. A major target of the country's extreme xenophobia – defined as a heightened form of xenophobia in which hostility and opposition to those perceived as outsiders and foreigners is expressed through violent acts – is the businesses run by migrants and refugees in the informal sector. Attitudinal surveys clearly show that South Africans differentiate migrants by national origin and that Zimbabweans are amongst the most disliked. Zimbabweans are certainly not the only small-business owners to have become victims of extreme xenophobia. However, few studies to date have specifically examined the impact of xenophobic violence on Zimbabweans who are trying to make a living in the South African informal sector.

This report is based on two sources of data: (a) in 2015, SAMP's Growing Informal Cities (GIC) Project surveyed over 1,000 randomly selected migrant-owned informal sector enterprises in Cape Town and Johannesburg. The data on 304 Zimbabwean-owned enterprises included in the survey sample has been extracted for analysis; and (b) in 2016, 50 in-depth interviews were conducted with Zimbabwean informal business owners in Cape Town, Johannesburg and Polokwane who had been affected by xenophobic violence.

The demographic profile of the Zimbabwean migrant entrepreneurs in the GIC survey included the following:

- As many as 60% of Zimbabwean entrepreneurs in Cape Town and 65% in Johannesburg are male. This was a marked contrast to informal cross-border trade between Zimbabwe and South Africa, which is dominated by female Zimbabweans.

- The number of migrant entrepreneurs who arrived in South Africa peaked between 2005 and 2010 at the height of the economic crisis in Zimbabwe and has since fallen. As many as 88% of the migrants in Cape Town arrived in the city after 2005 (compared to 52% of those in Johannesburg).

- Only 5% of the survey respondents had experience working in the Zimbabwean informal economy before migrating to South Africa. Those with prior experience had generally been involved in informal cross-border trading and were therefore familiar with South Africa.

- Relatively few of the Zimbabwean entrepreneurs did not have documents permitting them to be in the country and/or to work legally. Just over one-third of the migrants in the survey had asylum-seeker (Section 22) permits but only 5% had refugee status (Section 24 permits). Around one-quarter had work permits and 10% had visitor's permits. Only 15% did not have permits to reside and/or work in South Africa.

The majority of the surveyed Zimbabwean enterprises were in the retail, trade and wholesale sector, followed by services and manufacturing. Most migrants did not start an informal business immediately on arrival in South Africa but first raised start-up capital through regular and casual employment.

Against this backdrop, the report focuses on the findings from the in-depth interviews with Zimbabwean entrepreneurs. First, we review their experience of xenophobia and xenophobic violence. Most of the respondents recounted incidents of violence that had personally affected them. These accounts revealed a number of common features:

- To migrants, much of the violence occurs without warning and appears spontaneous. However, this is rarely the case as many attacks are preceded by community meetings from which migrants are excluded. They, therefore, have little ability or time to take evasive action.

- The perpetrators of xenophobic violence are often from the same community and are even personally known to their victims. The fact that migrant entrepreneurs provide goods, including food, at competitive prices and offer credit to consumers is clearly insufficient to protect them when violence erupts. In many areas, community leaders are ineffective in dealing with the violence and, in some cases, they actively foment hostility and instigate attacks.

- The looting of stock on the premises is a constant feature of the attacks. However, robbery per se is not the prime motive for the attacks. Virtually all agreed that the purpose of the attacks was not simply to steal certain desirable goods but to destroy their business premises and operations so that they could not continue to operate and would go back to Zimbabwe.

- South African business owners in the same vicinity are left alone during crowd violence.

- Attacks often involve vicious physical assaults against the person, accompanied by insulting xenophobic language.

- Many accounts describe how anti-government service delivery protests quickly disintegrate into mob violence and looting of shops owned by migrants. The looting is never indiscriminate and targets only migrants. Migrants feel that they are scapegoats for government failure to deliver services.

- There was some evidence of "violent entrepreneurship" involving attacks orchestrated by South African competitors.

- Xenophobic violence is gender-indiscriminate with male and female migrants recounting equally harrowing stories.

- The respondents differed on whether Zimbabweans were particular targets. Most said that all foreign-owned businesses were targeted. A number commented that the type of business made a difference, with food and grocery shops being especially vulnerable.

The pervasive view amongst South African politicians is that xenophobia does not exist in the country. However, the term "xenophobia" was used by all the respondents to describe the harassment and physical abuse that they experience and some even referred to the widespread violence in 2008 and 2015 as "the xenophobia." The language and practices of xenophobia cow the victims into silence and a sense of helplessness. The interviews provide important insights into how migrant entrepreneurs respond to the threat and reality of xenophobic violence. Trying to "fit in" and integrate by learning local languages, dress codes and cultural practices is one way to try to pre-empt attacks. However, these strategies are no guarantee of protection when mob violence breaks out. Some suggested that there was safety in numbers and that conducting business in areas where there were many other migrant businesses reduced the risks of being attacked. The downside of operating in safer spaces is that business competition is extremely fierce.

Most are aware that a great deal of the xenophobic violence is confined to low-income areas, particularly informal settlements. While it is possible for some to avoid doing business in these areas, and to operate in areas of the city where attacks are less frequent, this is not feasible for all. Many Zimbabwean migrants to South Africa do not have the financial means to afford accommodation outside informal settlements and do not have the resources to run a business elsewhere.

Several respondents noted that the unpredictability of the attacks made it difficult to plan in advance. Some said that they made sure that they did not keep all of their stock at the place of business, storing some at home or in rented containers. All tried to minimize the amount of cash they kept on the premises. Various reactive strategies were mentioned, including temporarily ceasing business operations, staying indoors at home, and moving in with friends or relatives in other parts of the city.

None of the respondents said that xenophobic attacks would put them permanently out of business. On the contrary, most said that they would simply raise the capital and start again. The logical implication of this is that xenophobic violence fails in its two main aims: to drive migrant entrepreneurs out of business and to drive them out of the country. Many respondents made reference to the fact that the crisis in Zimbabwe meant that there was nothing for them to return to, even if they wanted to return.

"Here we live with xenophobia every day. We see it happening and there is nothing that we can do" (Zimbabwean Migrant, Johannesburg, August 2016)

INTRODUCTION

South Africa's crisis of xenophobia in South Africa is defined by the daily discrimination and intolerance to which migrants are exposed. Xenophobia manifests in "a broad spectrum of behaviours including discriminatory, stereotyping and dehumanizing remarks; discriminatory policies and practices by government and private officials such as exclusion from public services to which target groups are entitled; selective enforcement of by-laws by local authorities; assault and harassment by state agents particularly the police and immigration officials; as well as public threats and violence…that often results in massive loss of lives and livelihoods."[1] The nub of the crisis of xenophobia in South Africa is when feelings of hostility and intolerance manifest as extreme xenophobia, which has been defined as "a heightened form of xenophobia in which hostility and opposition to those perceived as outsiders and foreigners is strongly embedded and expressed through aggressive acts directed at migrants and refugees (and) recurrent episodes of violence."[2]

SAMP's national surveys have consistently found that a significant minority of South African citizens are willing to resort to violence to rid their communities of migrants.[3] The deadliest examples of extreme xenophobia in South Africa were high-profile and widespread violence against migrants and refugees in May 2008 and March 2015. The nature and impacts of the 2008 violence are now well documented, although there remain differences of opinion about its causes.[4] Analyses of May 2008 tend to treat the victims of xenophobic violence in an undifferentiated fashion, leading to the assumption that all migrants – irrespective of national origin, legal status, length of time in the country and livelihood activity – were equally at risk. Yet, attitudinal surveys clearly show that South Africans differentiate migrants by national origin and that Zimbabweans are amongst the most disliked.[5] Discussions of May 2008 also do not differentiate sufficiently between the types of targets that were attacked. For example, many African migrants and refugees operated small businesses in the informal economy of affected urban areas and these enterprises came under sustained attack. In the 2015 xenophobic attacks, informal businesses run by migrants and refugees were explicitly targeted. Violent attacks on migrant and refugee entrepreneurs and their businesses have not been confined to acute episodes of extreme xenophobia such as in May 2008 and March 2015.[6] Extreme xenophobia increasingly manifests in the form of collective violence targeting migrant and refugee-owned businesses.

The frequency and ferocity of such attacks have increased over time and cannot simply be written off, as the state seeks to do, as "mere criminality." Chronic extreme xenophobia has prompted various responses and remedial actions by migrants and refugees, including paying protection money, beefing up business security, arming in self-defence, avoiding neighbourhoods known to be particularly dangerous, and moving away from the major cities to smaller urban centres.[7] Zimbabweans are certainly not the only small-business owners affected by extreme xenophobia in South Africa and attacks on migrants and refugees from other countries are well documented.[8] However, few studies to date have specifically examined the impact of xenophobic violence on Zimbabweans who are trying to make a living in the South African informal sector.[9]

This report is based on two sources of data. First, in 2015 SAMP's Growing Informal Cities (GIC) Project surveyed over 1,000 randomly selected migrant-owned informal sector enterprises in Cape Town and Johannesburg. The results of this survey have been discussed in previous SAMP reports.[10] The survey sample included 304 Zimbabwean-owned enterprises. For the purposes of this report, we extracted this data for analysis. Second, 50 in-depth interviews were conducted in 2016 with Zimbabwean informal business owners in Cape Town, Johannesburg and Polokwane.

MIGRATION FOR SURVIVAL

The exodus from Zimbabwe has been labelled an example of "survival migration," defined as a combination of refugees and "people who are forced to cross an international border to flee state failure, severe environmental distress, or widespread livelihood collapse."[11] Under conditions of survival migration, the traditional distinction between refugees and economic migrants breaks down.[12] The argument that all Zimbabwean migrants should be defined as "survival migrants" requires closer scrutiny. For example, it is based in part on the view that conditions in Zimbabwe are so bad that out-migration for survival is the only option. However, this does not explain why the majority of Zimbabweans have not left nor the role of migration in reducing pressures for further out-migration through remittances.[13]

The argument that all Zimbabweans are "survival migrants" also runs the danger of homogenizing migrant flows and downplaying the heterogeneity of migration movement out of the country. The idea that migrants from Zimbabwe are "survival migrants" also seems to rest on the desperate situation of migrants in squalid transit shelters in the border town of Musina and at overcrowded safe havens such as churches.[14] The idea of "survival migration" may fit here but it certainly does not encompass all migrants. Far from being the destitute and hapless people conveyed by the image of "survival migration," many Zimbabwean migrants to South Africa exhibit considerable ingenuity, industry and energy.

A recent survey of Zimbabwean migrants in Cape Town and Johannesburg found that over 60% of migrants who had come to South Africa in the previous decade were in formal employment and only 18% were unemployed.[15] At the same time, increasing numbers were doing more menial jobs with 25% in manual work, 13% in the service industry and 8% in domestic work. A longitudinal study of day labourers in Tshwane demonstrates that the proportion of Zimbabweans seeking casual work rose from 7% in 2004 to 33% in 2007 to 45% of workseekers in 2015.[16]

The true extent of participation by Zimbabwean migrants in the South African informal sector is unknown, but there are some indications. SAMP's 2005 national survey of migrant-sending households in Zimbabwe, for example, found that 21% of working migrants outside the country were in the informal sector.[17] A 2007 survey of migrants in Johannesburg found that 19% were working as hawkers or artisans.[18] SAMP's 2010 survey of recent Zimbabwean migrants in Johannesburg and Cape Town found that 27% were working or deriving income from the informal sector.[19] AFSUN's 2015 survey of poorer Zimbabwean households in South Africa found that 36% of household members in employment were working in the informal economy.[20] While indicative, these studies suggest that between 20-30% of Zimbabwean migrants in major South African cities could be involved in the informal economy. They also suggest that the importance of informal sector employment to Zimbabweans has increased over time.

The 2015 SAMP survey of migrant enterprises found a distinct gender bias in both cities with 60% of Zimbabwe entrepreneurs in Cape Town and 65% in Johannesburg being male. This was a marked contrast to the business of informal cross-border trading between Zimbabwe and South Africa, which is dominated by Zimbabwean women.[21] The number of migrant entrepreneurs who arrived in South Africa peaked between 2005 and 2010 at the height of the economic crisis in Zimbabwe and appears to have fallen since (Figure 1). Less than 2% had moved to South Africa before 1994. Nearly 18% of the Johannesburg migrant entrepreneurs had moved there before 2000 compared to only 2% of those in Cape Town. Over time, Cape Town has therefore become an increasingly attractive destination. As many as 88% of the migrants in Cape Town arrived in the city after 2005 (compared to 52% of those who moved to Johannesburg).

FIGURE 1: Comparison of Year of Migration and Year of Establishing Informal Business

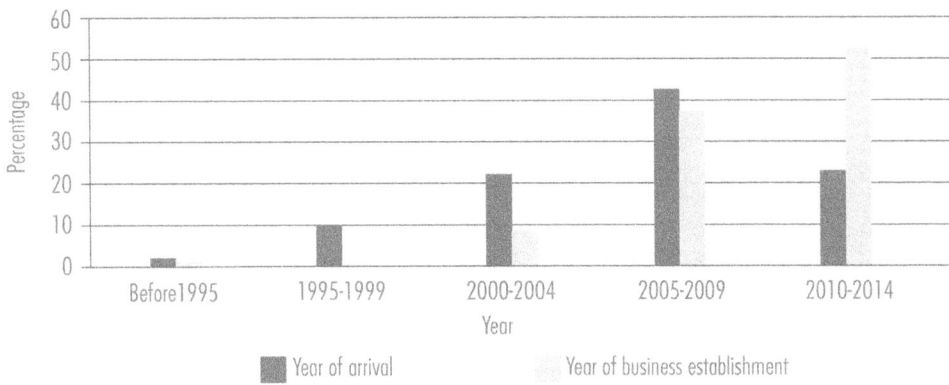

Only 5% of the survey respondents had worked in the informal economy in Zimbabwe before migrating to South Africa. Those with prior experience had generally been involved in informal cross-border trading and were therefore familiar with South Africa. One male migrant described the transition as follows:

> I used to come here as a trader from the early 2000s. I stopped in 2005 and came here to South Africa to live. My business is about making and selling electric jugs and brooms. I used to come here and sell them and go back home. There are some reasons why I came to stay. One is that the economic situation was getting bad. [Zimbabwe] was no longer the same. I was selling things and not making much money. I wanted to build a house in Zimbabwe and I was failing to do so. The cost of living was high. I had just married and things were tough. Then there was the issue of politics. My wife was harassed when I was in Johannesburg buying goods. They came and searched our house and they found nothing. They wanted evidence that I was a sell-out, but they did not find anything. My wife was pregnant so I saw that they could injure her if they came back next time. That is when I moved to South Africa (Johannesburg Interview No. 4, 15 August 2016).

In this case, economic hardship and political harassment were additional factors in the decision to move to South Africa. The overall reasons for migration to South Africa were clearly related to the ongoing economic crisis in Zimbabwe. Over 80% agreed with the proposition that that they had come to South Africa to provide for family back home. As many as 73% said that they had come to South Africa to look for employment (Figure 2). There was a marked difference here between the Johannesburg and Cape Town respondents (with 82% and 59% in agreement respectively) which may reflect differences in the perception (and reality) of labour market access in the two cities.

FIGURE 2: Reasons for Migrating to South Africa

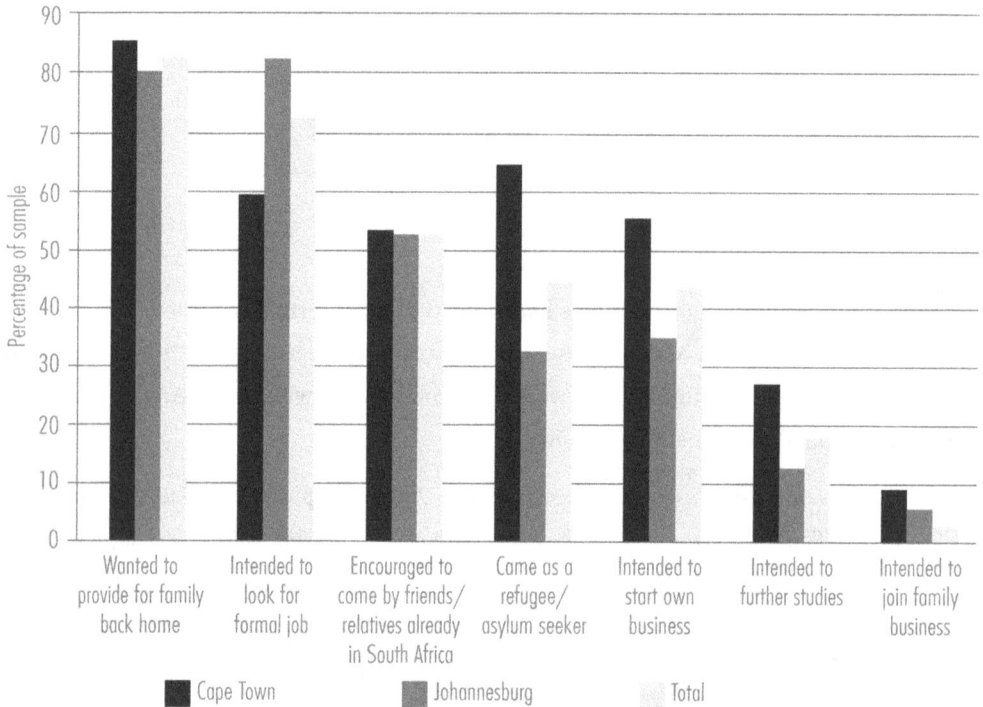

The reverse was true with regard to starting a business as a reason for migration, with 56% in Cape Town and 35% in Johannesburg in agreement. In general, this suggests that Johannesburg is seen as a place where it is easier to obtain formal sector employment and Cape Town is a more amenable location for starting an informal business. Unemployment was a significant driver of migration, with 39% of the sample reporting that they were unemployed prior to leaving Zimbabwe. Again, there was a marked difference between the entrepreneurs in the two cities: only 20% of the Cape Town respondents were unemployed before leaving compared with 51% of the Johannesburg respondents. The high proportion who said that they had migrated as refugees or asylum-seekers is a reflection of the fact that over 300,000 Zimbabweans applied for asylum-seeker permits between 2004 and 2010 in order to legalize their stay in South Africa.[22] At the same time, a proportion of this number left because of political persecution. Exactly how many is difficult to say given that South Africa has approved fewer than 3,000 of all Zimbabwean refugee claimants.

The survey found that relatively few of the Zimbabwean entrepreneurs did not have documents permitting them to be in the country and/or to work legally (Table 1). Just over one-third of the migrants had asylum-seeker (Section 22) permits but only 5% had refugee status (Section 24 permits). Both asylum-seekers and refugees have a legal right to work and earn. Around one-quarter had work permits, which the majority would have acquired under the Zimbabwe Dispensation Programme (ZDP) in 2010 and 2014.[23] Around 10% of the migrants had visitor's permits, which are usually issued for 90 days at a time. Only 15% were undocumented and did not have permits to reside and/or work in South Africa.

TABLE 1: Migration Status of Zimbabwean Entrepreneurs

	Total (%)	Cape Town (%)	Johannesburg (%)
Asylum-seeker permit	35.9	43.2	31.2
Work permit	24.7	17.8	29.0
Visitor's permit	9.5	8.5	10.2
Refugee permit	5.3	8.5	3.2
Permanent resident	4.6	3.4	5.4
Undocumented	14.5	16.1	13.4
Other	2.3	0.8	3.3
No answer	3.1	1.6	4.3

The majority of the surveyed Zimbabwean migrant enterprises were in the retail, trade and wholesale sector, followed by services and manufacturing, with slight differences between the two cities (Figure 3). As Figure 1 shows, most migrants did not start an informal business immediately on arrival in South Africa but first needed to raise start-up capital. Migrants and refugees face severe obstacles in accessing loans from formal sources in South Africa as they require collateral.[24] Just over three-quarters of the migrant entrepreneurs in this survey relied on their personal savings to start their business (Table 2). There was slightly greater reliance on personal savings by entrepreneurs in Johannesburg (87%) than Cape Town (64%). More Zimbabwean migrants in Cape Town were able to access funds from relatives and non-relatives.

FIGURE 3: Sectoral Breakdown of Zimbabwean Migrant Businesses

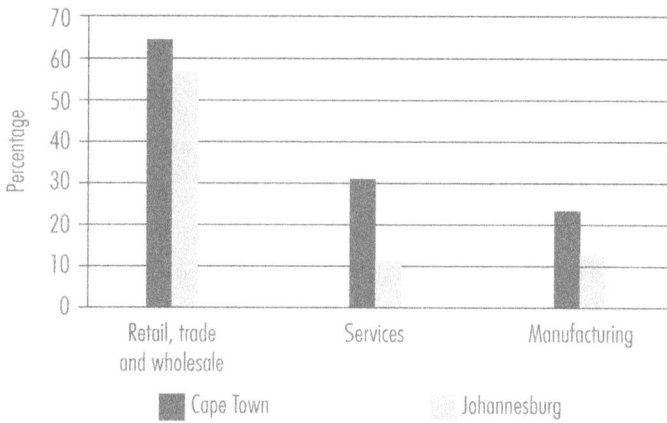

TABLE 2: Primary Sources of Start-Up Capital

	Total (%)	Cape Town (%)	Johannesburg (%)
Personal savings	78.0	64.4	86.6
Loan from relatives	9.2	13.6	6.5
Loan from non-relatives	6.6	15.3	1.1
Money lenders	2.0	1.7	2.2
Loan from informal financial institutions	2.0	1.7	2.2
Business credit (goods on terms)	0.7	0.0	1.1
Loan from micro-finance institution	0.3	0.8	0.0
Other source of capital	1.3	2.5	0.5

EXPERIENCING XENOPHOBIA

All of the Zimbabwean entrepreneurs interviewed in depth had either witnessed or been the victim of xenophobic violence or both. The interviews focused on the experience and impact of xenophobic violence on personal safety and business operations. Many of those interviewed had come to South Africa after the nationwide attacks on migrants in May 2008 but they all knew of the violence and many knew victims. Those who had been in the country at the time had lost almost everything, but they did not return permanently to Zimbabwe, which was a primary objective of their attackers. Instead, they took refuge in shelters and churches and rebuilt their businesses once the worst of the violence was over.

Three accounts in widely separated parts of the country (Alexandra Park in Johannesburg, Imizamo Yethu in Cape Town, and Mankweng in Polokwane) show both the destructive nature of the 2008 xenophobic violence and the responses of the migrants:

> During the xenophobic attacks of 2008 I was there. My musika was destroyed. People came marching and asking foreigners to leave…They came and destroyed the musika. It was made up of cardboard and corrugated iron sheets. They destroyed it. The cardboard was burnt and the corrugated sheets were taken and some of them thrown all over. I lost a lot of money there. Maybe ZAR3,000. I had a lot of goods and I was also selling beans, groundnuts and even matemba and fish. I lost everything. I was only able to carry a few things and fled. Otherwise they would have killed me as well. What could they do? The people that start the violence are the ones that can even kill you. Many people died in Alex Park. They died. I actually saw a person who had been stoned to death and he was lying there for a day without the police getting him (Johannesburg Interview No. 13, 14 August 2016).

> I had just closed my spaza and had not even reached home when I saw people singing and getting up here. They were coming from the direction of the police station, coming uphill. We had already heard of xenophobia and so I knew it was happening here. I wanted to go back and get some things from the spaza but I was too late because they were moving fast. I just had time to change direction and ended up in Hout Bay. There were other Zimbabweans who had also run away and were there. I joined them and we went to Wynberg and stayed there at the police station. There were many of us. Like me, most people had nothing because they never had time to go home and get clothes or blankets. I called someone in Rosebank and they told us that they were staying at a Methodist church there so that is where we went. We spent three weeks there. My spaza shop was looted. I never got anything back, not even a single sweet. They took everything so I had to start from scratch (Cape Town Interview No. 20, 15 October 2016).

> I was living in Mankweng with two other ladies from Zimbabwe. We were renting a room in Zone 2. We had been living there for some time and we knew most of the people there. But when xenophobia erupted it was as if we had never

lived there. We saw some of the people that we knew actually looting things belonging to foreigners. We were confronted by a group of young men – and they demanded money otherwise they would kill us. It was like a dream. We could not believe it. We were robbed there, close to the road, where everyone could see. They just took what they wanted and went away singing. I lost my bag, my wallet and my friend also lost everything. I was scared that we could be killed or raped. Even now I cannot believe that I survived. We went to the highway, the N1, and hiked to Musina and then home to Zimbabwe. I only came back after a month when things had calmed down. I stopped doing business for over a month. I had no money to start over. I had to borrow some money and it took time to recover. Some of my customers moved with my money and I never recovered the money. I had to start from scratch and it was difficult (Polokwane Interview No. 3, 11 September 2016).

Most of the respondents recounted incidents of violence since 2008 that had personally affected them. These accounts reveal a number of features common to xenophobic attacks on migrant businesses. First, from the migrants' perspective, much of the violence seems spontaneous and occurs without warning. As one victim of violence in the informal settlement of Diepsloot near Johannesburg in 2013 observed:

They just occur haphazardly. We cannot always tell what happens next so it is difficult do anything and to think of a way to respond. It just happens when you are least aware of the problems that are about to erupt. Sometimes we are caught up with all our wares and they are destroyed and stolen and so it is difficult to do anything (Johannesburg Interview No. 10, 16 August 2016).

Migrants therefore have little time or ability to take evasive action. A study of Diepsloot paints a picture of a volatile settlement in which vigilante justice and attacks on foreign-owned businesses are common.[25] In 2008, for example, "they showed no discrimination in targeting men, women and children, and destroyed, looted and burnt down their businesses and houses."[26]

Second, the perpetrators of xenophobic violence are often from the same community and personally known to the victims:

The people that robbed us are in this community and we know them. They are the community members here. Some of the people here do not like us foreigners.

They pretend when you deal with them to like us. But they do not like us (Johannesburg Interview No. 2, 15 August 2016).

The fact that migrant entrepreneurs provide goods, including food, at competitive prices and offer credit to consumers is clearly insufficient to protect them when violence erupts. In one part of Khayelitsha, for example, there is reportedly little violence as long as migrant business owners pay protection money to the powerful local taxi association. In many other areas, the respondents reported that community leaders are either ineffective in dealing with the violence or, in some cases, actively foment hostility and instigate attacks.

Third, the looting of stock on the premises is a constant feature in the narratives of the migrant business owners. As one observed:

There are hard-core thieves who rob people and also jobless people around who are now taking advantage of these xenophobic attacks and robbing people to get money because they have nothing to do with their lives (Johannesburg Interview No. 1, 14 August 2016).

However, the respondents consistently maintained that robbery per se was not the prime motive for the attacks. As one respondent noted:

They target shops – the owners as well as the goods inside. They only target foreign-owned shops. There is more to that (than robbery), they want us to leave their country because they hate our businesses here and they say we are finishing their jobs (Johannesburg Interview No. 3, 14 August 2016).

Others pointed out that South African business owners in the same vicinity are left alone during crowd violence, and that attacks often involve vicious physical assaults and are accompanied by vituperative xenophobic language:

People were being beaten up and they were dying. A group of South Africans moved around this whole squatter camp terrorizing all foreigners and they used to move with someone who knew where all foreigners stayed. These people moved with knobkerries, metal sticks, sjamboks and any sort of weapon you can think of for distraction. If you were a foreigner and did not have a passport they would beat you up (Johannesburg Interview No. 3, 14 August 2016).

> *The violence was there for two days or so and I thought it was over. I went to service a car in Heideveld. When I was coming back I passed through my friend's place and he accompanied me half way. When he had gone, and I was in Sisulu Street down there, they attacked me with a plank and something like a rubber. They hit me all over and even stomped on me. It was xenophobia. They told me that they would kill me and that I was a foreigner and not wanted here. I cried and asked for them to leave me and they continued. No one intervened. It was past 8pm and there were still people moving about. A few other guys joined in. I was saved by a car that passed, when its lights flashed at them they ran away. They told me that next time they would kill me (Cape Town Interview No. 3, 9 October 2016).*

> *I was robbed in broad daylight here in Masiphumelele. It was not a real robbery, it was a gang just saying foreigners must leave. I was about to park my car when the group of men descended on me. They asked for my ID and when I said let me go and get it, they pounced on me and started pushing me. My neighbours just looked on. I asked what I had done but they were just singing derogatory songs. It was pure xenophobia. Most of the locals here joined and wanted to chase me out. Even my neighbours were caught up in that chaos and were told to go. You see, when there is a small thing that happens, it ends up being that foreigners must be chased away. Is that not xenophobia? Many times here I have been insulted only because I am a foreigner. You ferry someone's goods and they pay you little and the next time you want your balance they start some story that you are a thief or so on and the others join in. Is that not xenophobia? Why do they not do that to South Africans? Why only to foreigners? These people have xenophobia in their blood (Cape Town Interview No. 12, 12 October 2016).*

Fourth, many of the accounts describe how anti-government service delivery protests or marches quickly disintegrate into mob violence and looting of shops owned by migrants. According to the respondents, the looting is never indiscriminate and targets only migrants. The reason, according to some, is that migrants become scapegoats for government failure to deliver services:

> *South Africans are not friendly. They say this is their country and they do what they want to us, hurting us. These locals ask services from their government and if they are not given them they demonstrate and if their concerns are not heard*

they put their frustrations on foreigners. Most of them are uneducated so they think we are the cause of their problem and when they see you in business they think you are taking over their business. They target foreigners in business. They start with businesses and sometimes when their concerns are not heard they even start attacking those not in business and foreigners in their homes (Cape Town Interview No. 11, 10 October 2016).

Fifth, there was some evidence of violent entrepreneurship involving attacks orchestrated by South African competitors. One Zimbabwean entrepreneur in Polokwane, for example, described how he had established a business selling and repairing cell phones. He said that his South African competitors reported him to the police for dealing in stolen phones but his records showed that all his transactions were legitimate. According to him, they had tried several times to get him arrested:

They even tell me to my face that they want me out of this place because I am a foreigner. How can they fail to make business when I as a foreigner am doing well? That is their quarrel. Some have even organized thieves to rob me and I have been robbed twice (Polokwane Interview No. 9, 16 August 2016).

Sixth, xenophobic violence is gender-indiscriminate in that both male and female migrants recounted equally harrowing stories. One of the most common strategies adopted by Zimbabwean women migrants travelling to South Africa as cross-border traders is to travel and stay in groups as a means of protection.[27] Zimbabwean women living in South Africa and selling on the streets are generally unable to benefit from group protection. One woman in Johannesburg described her experience and helpless situation as follows:

They were calling me names and some were telling me to go back to Zimbabwe, saying I would die that night. Some of the foreigners who were there and had been trying to support me saw that the situation was getting serious and just disappeared. I lost most of my goods that day as people just started taking them. The lady who was selling close to me also lost her products as people just took and went. It was terrible. No one was on our side. They just did not care that we were females. They just harassed us. I even thought of going back home that day. What stopped me is the thought of going back to look at my kids without anything. And there was nothing that I would do in Zimbabwe (Johannesburg Interview No. 10, 16 August 2016).

Finally, the respondents differed on whether Zimbabweans were particular targets. Most said that all foreign-owned businesses were targeted. A number commented that the type of business made a difference, with food and grocery shops being especially vulnerable. However, virtually all agreed that the purpose of the attacks was not simply to steal certain desirable goods but to destroy their business premises and operations so that they could not continue to operate. There were numerous examples of entrepreneurs who had lost all of their stock and also had their premises vandalized and wrecked, even when they were operating from containers, which are generally considered to be the best form of protection:

> They broke and took away everything as if they don't want one to be in business. If they wanted goods only, they would have just broken in and taken stuff only but they destroyed, breaking windows and even removing them and most people are not yet back on their feet (Cape Town Interview No. 8, 7 July 2016).

> In 2011, the business was attacked by local people. The shop was attacked by the mob. They looted everything and left me with almost nothing. I had goods worth over ZAR15,000 in here. Everything except some few bottles of cooking oil and cigarettes remained. It almost destroyed my business. I was left with very little. I had not saved much so it took me some time to be on my feet again. I had to borrow some money from friends because I needed to restock. I cannot afford to stock much as I am not sure what happens tomorrow. These days we no longer put everything here. Some of the stock is at home so that if they steal here, I will have some of my stock at home to start again. I just replenish what is in short supply here (Cape Town Interview No. 10, 9 October 2016).

> We had just brought stuff from Zimbabweans on a Sunday. They were worth about ZAR10,000 and included nyimo, mbambaira, nzungu, matemba and we had also just stocked the local products. We had bought a lot of crates like onions for about ZAR15,000. All these products were in the container and the container was destroyed. They upended it and spilled all the products that were inside to the ground. Some of the products were burnt, taken and we were left with nothing. And because we had just stocked we didn't have any money at home so we had to start all over from scratch (Cape Town Interview No. 1, 7 July 2016).

RESPONSES TO XENOPHOBIC VIOLENCE

The pervasive view amongst South African politicians is that xenophobia does not exist in the country. However, the term "xenophobia" was used by all the respondents to describe the harassment and physical abuse that they experience and some even referred to the widespread violence in 2008 and 2015 as "the xenophobia." They were asked if they thought South Africans were xenophobic and, if so, why. None answered the question in the negative. A selection of responses clearly indicate that, for Zimbabweans, South Africans are intensely xenophobic:

> I can say that three-quarters of them show their hatred towards us foreign nationals. They don't like us. Xenophobia is a South African thing. It happens more than anywhere in the world I think. Everything they do shows it. They do not like us. They speak to us like we are not like them. They look down upon us. They are like that whether they are Christians or not. The children learn it from their parents. They call us makwerekwere. Do you know even small kids can call you makwerekwere? Is that not xenophobic? (Johannesburg Interview No. 2, 15 August 2016).

> If you want to see how they hate us, just have a disagreement and they will tell you bad things, telling you that you will die. What kind of a person wants to see another person dying? Life is sacred, but here in South Africa no one seems to care about that. They would rather you die so that they can get what you have. This is the only society where people kill each other over very simple disagreements (Johannesburg Interview No. 10, 16 August 2016).

> You can see it almost every day in the train and other places – when you pass they call you derogatory names like makwerekwere. We can see it every day in our daily life and we live with it. It does not only happen to people doing business, but it happens to any foreigner no matter whom. If you can't speak their language, you already are a kwerekwere and you are in trouble (Cape Town Interview No. 4, 9 July 2016).

> The way they see us, they see us as if we are lesser than them. They say bad things about us, like we are thieves and we are ugly and we do not bath, such things. They know most of these things are not true but they like saying them anyway (Cape Town Interview No. 10, 9 October 2016).

Is there a country in the world where foreigners are killed and burnt like here? No. South Africa is a place like no other place. It is a country with people that do not care about other people. Look at the way they kill foreigners. The way they chase foreigners and steal their goods and injure them. That is not done by normal people. South Africans are xenophobic. They do not fear evil spirits from the dead. They just kill and the next hour they are busy braaiing and singing and eating amagwinya. They are not normal people (Cape Town Interview No. 12, 14 October 2016).

The language and practices of xenophobia cow the victims into silence and a sense of helplessness: "I remain silent because I am Zimbabwean and I can't go against what they say. But they have to realize that we are the same, we have the same skin as black people but we just keep quiet even as they insult us" (Johannesburg Interview No. 12, 14 August 2016).

The interviews provide important insights into how migrant entrepreneurs themselves respond to the threat and reality of xenophobic violence. From the responses of some of the migrants, it appears that trying to "fit in" and integrate by learning local languages, dress codes and cultural practices is one way to try to pre-empt attacks.[28] However, these strategies are no guarantee of protection when mob violence breaks out:

I was robbed during the day. There was a strike and I was coming from the shops. I was not here the previous day and so I did not know that there was a strike. When they saw me coming the mob ran to me. I was beaten and robbed. They knew I was a foreigner. I can speak three local languages and I spoke in isiZulu but they knew me, some of them and they said he is a Zimbabwean and they attacked me. If I was a local I was not going to be attacked. I had ZAR1,800. All was taken. That was my money that I had collected from my customers. They robbed me because I was a Zimbabwean, a foreigner (Johannesburg Interview No. 2, 15 August 2016).

A number of the respondents observed that, unlike some migrant groups such as Somalis and Ethiopians, Zimbabweans are not inclined to band together to form associations or groups to lobby for and secure protection for their members. Some did suggest that there was safety in numbers and that doing business in areas with many other migrant businesses considerably reduced the risk of being attacked. One respondent explained the attraction of running a business in the Johannesburg CBD as follows: "You will find that incidents of xenophobic attacks are very rare in Jo'burg central where there are a lot of foreigners. Also, Park Station is a strategic location which supplies the whole of South Africa so our protection as foreigners is better" (Johannesburg Interview No. 13, 14 August 2016). The downside of operating in safer spaces is that business competition is extremely fierce.

Most were aware that a great deal of the xenophobic violence is confined to low-income areas, particularly informal settlements. While it was possible for some to avoid doing business in these areas, and instead operate in areas of the city where attacks are less frequent, this was not a feasible option for all. Many Zimbabwean migrants to South Africa are unable to afford accommodation or to run their businesses anywhere other than informal settlements.

A number of the respondents noted that the unpredictability of the attacks made it difficult to plan in advance. Some said that they made sure that they did not keep all of their stock at the place of business, and stored some of it at home or in rented containers. All tried to minimize the amount of cash they kept on the premises, although not many Zimbabwean entrepreneurs have access to formal banking facilities. One noted that as soon as he had made some money, he remitted it to Zimbabwe immediately, "so that even if I am attacked, there is nothing much that they can take from me. It is better if my family can have that money" (Polokwane Interview No. 6, 13 August 2016). Another said that he was planning to relocate once he had saved sufficient capital:

> I am thinking of saving a lot of money and looking for safer business locations like in town. I am thinking so because in 2008 they also attacked my business. They just broke and took away all my stuff; now they have burnt the structure down. So I re-constructed and started again, so I am now thinking how I am to keep myself and my stuff safe (Cape Town Interview No. 15, 14 October 2016).

Various reactive strategies for dealing with attacks on businesses were mentioned, including temporarily ceasing operations, staying indoors at home, and moving in with friends or relatives in other parts of the city "until the dust settled" as one put it. Others said that the best strategy was to flee the area ("you run with your life," said one) and, if possible, take a valuable item that could be sold to enable restarting the business. None of the respondents said that xenophobic attacks would put them permanently out of business. On the contrary, most said that they would simply raise the capital and start again.

The logical implication of the determination to stay in business is that xenophobic violence has failed in its two main aims: to drive migrant entrepreneurs out of business and to drive them out of the country. The respondents were asked if they would return to Zimbabwe as a result of xenophobic attacks and the general consensus was that they would not. A significant number noted that they had settled in South Africa with their families and did not want to return. Many more made reference to the fact that the crisis in Zimbabwe meant that there was nothing for them to return to, even if they wished to do so:

> There is nothing in Zimbabwe. I am not going back. I am trying to make my life here. My wife is here and my child is here. I am not going back there. Zimbabwe is a country I love. It's just that at the moment things are tough and there is really nothing to do when you return back home (Johannesburg Interview No. 11, 14 August 2016).

> While the hardships which I face in South Africa are many they are still better than the hardships I endured back in Zimbabwe. In the event of future attacks, I could try and survive because at least I will be doing something (Johannesburg Interview No. 13, 14 August 2016).

> I could never go back because there are no means of surviving. I would simply have to look for an alternative way to survive while in South Africa. Even if they attack me I will look for another means to survive as long as I am not dead (Johannesburg Interview No. 19, 17 August 2016).

> I am not going back. There is nothing to do in Zimbabwe especially because we left a long time ago. What will we do there? So we stay here because this is where our life is. We are establishing here and so if you leave you have to start again. I am not going back. When xenophobia starts we simply move to areas that are safe and return when it is quiet (Cape Town Interview No. 7, 12 July 2016).

PERCEPTIONS OF GOVERNMENT INACTION

All respondents were asked about the response of the South African and Zimbabwean governments to xenophobic violence. The responses ranged from the cynical to the totally dismissive. Not a single respondent had been helped by either government and none was prepared to defend either government's response to xenophobic violence. Most were extremely critical of both governments. The general consensus was not that the governments did not do enough but rather that they did nothing at all. In the case of the Zimbabwean government, the prevailing sentiment was captured by one Johannesburg respondent who said:

> *The Zimbabwean government does nothing. I have never heard them comment or say anything about these attacks. They do not help us at all. They do not send anyone to come and see how we are living and even provide us with assistance. There is no government that helps us (Johannesburg Interview No. 2, 15 August 2016).*

Explanations for why the government "does nothing" included sheer lack of interest in what happens to Zimbabweans outside the country, a lack of resources to do anything to help, and a desire to see Zimbabweans return home instead of staying in South Africa.

Much harsher criticism was reserved for the South African government's practice of "doing nothing":

> *The South African government does not do anything. At least nothing that I know of. They are just silent (Johannesburg Interview No. 2, 15 August 2016).*

> *Some of the people in government are fuelling xenophobia. They are also xenophobic because they say a lot of things that are not true. Like we are the ones who are causing problems here. They had problems here before we came. They are very corrupt but they are the ones that tell people that foreigners are the cause of the problems. People listen to the government. They keep saying that foreigners are bad. What do you expect the people to do? The people follow their government (Cape Town Interview No. 5, 10 July 2016).*

> *They are the ones that cause it so they do not care. The one that occurred in Durban – it was the King who incited people. Now he is saying he did not do it but we all saw him on TV. The government does not care for us. They care about their people only. If it were foreigners doing violence against the locals, we would all be in jail (Cape Town Interview No. 6, 11 July 2016).*

Some felt that xenophobic violence was tolerated by government because it supposedly achieved the desired effect of getting "foreigners" to leave South Africa.

A recurring theme was police inaction during episodes of mass xenophobic violence. Some felt that the police were extremely slow to respond. One respondent noted that "the police usually come late when everything has been done and people have been killed or their goods stolen" (Cape Town Interview No. 5, 10 July 2016). Others commented on how, even when they were present, the police offered no protection:

> Both the City of Cape Town and the police are not protecting us at all. Like on the day that the people were demonstrating, the police were there. They were just walking. After they were passing, the people started taking our things. There was no one to protect us and no one to stop those people. So, I don't know what they are doing. I think they just put on uniforms and walk around. When there is trouble they don't come to protect us (Cape Town Interview No. 4, 9 July 2016).

> The police just stand at the robots [traffic lights]. Or they run away. There is poor enforcement because their response is very slow. Containers were being opened and things taken while the police stared. They are either scared of the people or because it's their own people so they can't stop them. There were three police vehicles, but they just stood while people's containers were being opened. Only foreign containers were broken and they knew whose container it is. No containers for local Xhosas (South Africans) were broken into and destroyed (Cape Town Interview No. 12, 12 October 2016).

One respondent felt that the reason for inaction was that "South Africans do not fear police" and compared the police behaviour with that in Zimbabwe:

> They throw stones at the police. Have you ever seen people throwing stones at the police in Zimbabwe? No, they do not do that. Here they just do what they want. So they attack foreigners even if the police are there. Unless the police are using teargas or throwing water. But they rarely do that. But you can run to a police station if you are close and seek refuge. There are other areas where the local people even attacked police stations – attacked foreigners in police stations (Cape Town Interview No. 7, 12 July 2016).

There was also a pervasive view, based on experiences, that there was little point reporting theft or assault to the police because nothing would be done. Dockets might be opened but the perpetrators were rarely arrested and brought to book and stolen goods were rarely, if ever, recovered:

> It was the mob that took the things and what would I tell the police? Besides, there were so many people whose goods were destroyed that I never bothered. The police do not help much. It is useless to report to the police. The police here

> *do not care. Especially if you are a foreigner. They will just tell you it is a mob.*
> *They cannot arrest a mob (Johannesburg Interview No. 2, 15 August 2016).*

The argument that the police were not particularly concerned about what happened to "foreigners" was very common.

> *We just see the police, but they come too late and do not do anything. They do*
> *not arrest anyone even though you report. They are just moving about, but really*
> *doing nothing. I sometimes think that even the police hate us the foreigners.*
> *Would they do the same and not help if foreigners attack local people? No,*
> *they would arrest us. So the police do not help us and would rather see us gone*
> *(Johannesburg Interview No. 2, 15 August 2016).*

One respondent claimed that even when a perpetrator was arrested, "as soon as they have gone around the corner they will ask for a bribe and release the person. As soon as the person is released they will either come and shoot you or permanently injure you" (Johannesburg Interview No. 18, 17 August 2016). Another respondent had reported a robbery to the police and even named the assailants but little was done:

> *They took down my details and the details of the things I lost. I listed all of them*
> *and went with them to the police station. I was told that they would call me*
> *when they have made progress and that was that. I went back but there was no*
> *progress. The officer who was dealing with the issue kept telling me there were no*
> *suspects and that there was nothing they could do. I even gave them some names*
> *of the suspects because I had seen some of them, but the police officer did not*
> *even take them down. He insisted that there needed to be a witness for him to*
> *put those people as witnesses. I thought he should have at least questioned them*
> *or gone to their homes and searched. Neither was done (Polokwane Interview*
> *No. 4, 12 August 2016).*

Apart from the failure to protect, in a xenophobic environment in which migrants are extremely vulnerable, police officers themselves might seek to take advantage of the situation for personal gain. This was certainly the view of many of the respondents who described persistent police harassment, and even theft, during business hours:

> *They know that we are not South Africans. Sometimes the metro and police*
> *can just come and take your products. During winter they came and took socks*
> *and hats. Once you just try to confront them, they tell you that this is not your*

country, go back to your country. Tomorrow the same thing can happen again. The police officer will just come and say they lost the gloves and take another pair. If that day they are in the mood of arresting people, they will arrest you despite the fact that they took your things before. Some are those who arrest you and ask for a certain amount of money like ZAR200 even if you don't have it. Maybe that day you only made ZAR50 and if you try to explain that you don't have the money, they threaten to take all your stock. If the stock value is more than ZAR200 and I don't have it, I am forced to ask from other people. If they assist me, I give them and they go and if not, they take all my stock (Johannesburg Interview No. 1, 14 August 2016).

Confiscation of stock appears to be relatively common and the owners are forced to pay large fines to retrieve their goods. In many cases, the fines are so heavy that they simply abandon the goods, borrow money and begin again. Simply to be allowed to operate in an area for a day or to avoid impounding of goods may require payment of a bribe of up to ZAR200. Mobile vendors play a continuous cat-and-mouse game with the police, ready to pack up their goods and disappear at the first sign of a police car. In sum, police protection cannot be counted on during episodes of mob violence and there is also very little redress when individuals report crimes against their businesses or themselves to the police. Fear of reprisals from those whom they report or identify is also a very real disincentive to getting the police involved. As a result, there is a certain fatalism to the inevitability of losing goods and property in general or isolated attacks.

CONCLUSION

There are three main policy and scholarly responses to violence against migrants in general, and migrant entrepreneurs in particular: xenophobia denialism (the official position of the South African government since 2008 and supported by some researchers who argue that South Africans are equally as vulnerable to violence as migrants); xenophobia minimalism (whose proponents suggest that xenophobia may exist but it is an epiphenomenon and that the real causes lie elsewhere); and xenophobia realism (which argues that xenophobia is not only widespread and real but can take a violent form in specific places and under certain circumstances).[29] This report revisits these arguments from the perspective of a group of migrants themselves; that is, Zimbabweans running businesses in the informal sector. The migrants have no difficulty in naming what happens to them as xenophobic. Their accounts clearly demonstrate that they see xenophobia as a key driver of the hostility, looting and violence that they experience. This report suggests that xenophobic violence has several key and common characteristics that put Zimbabwean informal enterprise owners at constant risk of losing their livelihoods and their lives. The deep-rooted crisis in Zimbabwe, which has driven many to South Africa in the first place, also makes return home a non-viable option. Instead, Zimbabweans are forced to adopt several self-protection strategies, none of which is ultimately an insurance against xenophobic attack.

ENDNOTES

1   Misago et al. (2015: 17).

2   Crush et al. (2015a).

3   Crush (2008); Crush et al. (2013).

4   Bekker (2015); Cabane (2015); Desai (2015); Everatt (2011); Hassim et al. (2008); Hayem (2013); Landau (2012); Steinberg (2012).

5   Crush et al. (2013).

6   Charman and Piper (2012); Crush et al. (2015); Crush and Ramachandran (2015a, 2015b); Tevera (2013).

7   Crush et al. (2015a).

8   Gastrow (2013); Gastrow and Amit (2015); Piper and Charman (2016).

9   Duri (2016); Hungwe, (2014); Sibanda and Sibanda (2014).

10 Peberdy (2016); Tawodzera et al. (2016).

11 Betts and Kaytaz (2009: 2).

12 Betts (2013).

13 Crush and Tevera (2010).

14 Betts and Kaytaz (2009); Kuljian (2013).

15 Crush et al. (2015b).

16 Blaauw et al. (2016).

17 Crush and Tevera (2010: 12).

18 Makina (2010).

19 Crush et al. (2015a).

20 Crush and Tawodzera (2017).

21 Chikanda and Tawodzera (2017).

22 Amit and Kriger (2014).

23 Thebe (2016).

24 Tawodzera et al. (2015).

25 Harber (2011).

26 Harber (2011: 123).

27 Lefko-Everett (2010).

28 Hungwe (2012, 2013).

29 Crush and Ramachandran (2014).

REFERENCES

1. Amit, R. and Kriger, N. (2014). "Making Migrants 'Il-legible': The Policies and Practices of Documentation in Post-Apartheid South Africa" *Kronos* 40: 269-290.

2. Bekker, S. (2015). "Violent Xenophobic Episodes in South Africa, 2008 and 2015" *African Human Mobility Review* 1: 229-252.

3. Betts, A. (2013). *Survival Migration: Failed Governance and the Crisis of Displacement* (Ithaca, NY: Cornell University Press).

4. Betts, A. and Kaytaz, E. (2009). "National and International Responses to the Zimbabwean Exodus: Implications for the Refugee Protection Regime" UNHCR Research Paper No. 175, Geneva.

5. Blaauw, D., Pretorius, A. and Schenck, R. (2016). "Day Labourers and the Role of Foreign Migrants: For Better or For Worse?" *Econ 3x3* May.

6. Cabane, L. (2015). "Protecting the 'Most Vulnerable'? The Management of a Disaster and the Making/Unmaking of Victims after the 2008 Xenophobic Violence in South Africa" *International Journal of Conflict and Violence* 9: 56-71.

7. Charman, A. and Piper, L. (2012). "Xenophobia, Criminality and Violent Entrepreneurship: Violence Against Somali Shopkeepers in Delft South, Cape Town, South Africa" *South African Review of Sociology* 43: 81-105.

8. Chikanda, A. and Tawodzera, G. (2017). *Informal Entrepreneurship and Informal Cross-Border Trade Between Zimbabwe and South Africa*. SAMP Migration Policy Series No. 74, Cape Town.

9. Crush, J. (2008). *The Perfect Storm: The Realities of Xenophobia in Contemporary South Africa*. SAMP Migration Policy Series No. 50, Cape Town.

10. Crush, J. and Ramachandran, S. (2014). *Xenophobic Violence in South Africa: Denialism, Minimalism, Realism*. SAMP Migration Policy Series No. 64, Cape Town.

11. Crush, J. and Ramachandran, S. (2015a). "Migration Myths and Extreme Xenophobia in South Africa" In D. Arcarazo and A. Wiesbrock (Eds.), *Global Migration: Old Assumptions, New Dynamics* (Santa Barbara, CA: Praeger), pp. 71-96.

12. Crush, J. and Ramachandran, S. (2015b). "Doing Business with Xenophobia" In J. Crush, A. Chikanda and C. Skinner (Eds.), *Mean Streets: Migration, Xenophobia and Informality in South Africa* (Ottawa: IDRC), pp. 25-59.

13. Crush, J. and Tawodzera, G. (2017). "South-South Migration and Urban Food Security: Zimbabwean Migrants in South African Cities" *International Migration* (in press).

14. Crush, J. and Tevera, D. (Eds.) (2010). *Zimbabwe's Exodus: Crisis, Migration, Survival* (Ottawa: IDRC).

15. Crush, J., Chikanda, A. and Skinner, C. (Eds.) (2015a). *Mean Streets: Migration, Xenophobia and Informality in South Africa* (Ottawa: IDRC).

16. Crush, J., Chikanda, A. and Tawodzera, G. (2015b). "The Third Wave: Mixed Migration from Zimbabwe to South Africa" *Canadian Journal of African Studies* 49: 363-382.

17. Crush, J., Ramachandran, S. and Pendleton, W. (2013). *Soft Targets: Xenophobia, Public Violence and Changing Attitudes to Migrants in South Africa After May 2008*. SAMP Migration Policy Series No. 64, Cape Town.

18. Desai, A. (2015). "Migrants and Violence in South Africa: The April 2015 Xenophobic Attacks in Durban" *Oriental Anthropologists* 15: 247-259.

19. Duri, F. (2016). "From Victims to Agents: Zimbabweans and Xenophobic Violence in Post-Apartheid South Africa" In M. Mawere and N. Marongwe (Eds.), *Myths of Peace and Democracy?* (Bamenda: RPCIG), pp. 21-60.

20. Everatt, D. (2011). "Xenophobia, State and Society in South Africa, 2008-2010" *Politikon* 38: 7-36.

21. Gastrow, V. (2013). "Business Robbery, The Foreign Trader and the Small Shop: How Business Robberies Affect Somali Traders in the Western Cape" *SA Crime Quarterly* 43: 5-16.

22. Gastrow, V. and Amit, R. (2016). "The Role of Migrant Traders in Local Economies: A Case Study of Somali Spaza Shops in Cape Town" In J. Crush, A. Chikanda and C. Skinner (Eds.), *Mean Streets: Migration, Xenophobia and Informality in South Africa* (Ottawa: IDRC), pp. 162-177.

23. Harber, A. 2011. *Diepsloot* (Jeppestown: Jonathan Ball).

24. Hassim, S., Kupe, T. and Worby, E. (Eds.) (2008). *Go Home or Die Here: Violence, Xeno-phobia and the Reinvention of Difference in South Africa* (Johannesburg: Wits University Press).

25. Hayem, J. (2013). "From May 2008 to 2011: Xenophobic Violence and National Subjec-tivity in South Africa" *Journal of Southern African Studies* 39: 77–97.

26. Hendow, M., Pailey, R. and Bravi, A. (2016). "Migrants in Countries in Crisis: A Com-parative Study of Six Crisis Situations" Report for International Centre for Migration Policy Development, ICMPD, Vienna.

27. Hungwe, C. (2012). "The Migration Experience and Multiple Identities of Zimbabwean Migrants in South Africa" *Journal of Social Research* 1: 132-138.

28. Hungwe, C. (2013). "Surviving Social Exclusion: Zimbabwean Migrants in Johannes-burg, South Africa" PhD Thesis, University of South Africa, Pretoria.

29. Hungwe, C. (2014). "Zimbabwean Migrant Entrepreneurs in Kempton Park and Tem-bisa, Johannesburg: Challenges and Opportunities" *Journal of Enterprising Culture* 22.

30. Kuljian, C. 2013. *Sanctuary* (Auckland Park: Jacana).

31. Landau, L. (Ed.) (2012). *Exorcising the Demons Within: Xenophobia, Violence and State-craft in Contemporary South Africa* (Johannesburg: Wits University Press).

32. Lefko-Everett, K. (2010). "The Voices of Migrant Zimbabwean Women in South Africa" In J. Crush and D. Tevera (Eds.), *Zimbabwe's Exodus: Crisis, Migration, Survival* (Ottawa: IDRC), pp. 269-290.

33. Makina, D. 2010. "Zimbabwe in Johannesburg" In J. Crush and D. Tevera (Eds.), *Zim-babwe's Exodus: Crisis, Migration, Survival* (Ottawa: IDRC), pp. 225-243.

34. Misago, J-P., Freemantle, I. and Landau, L. (2015). "Protection from Xenophobia: An Evaluation of UNHCR's Regional Office for Southern Africa's Xenophobia Related Pro-grammes" Report for UNHCR, Pretoria.

35. Peberdy, S. (2016). *International Migrants in Johannesburg's Informal Economy.* SAMP Migration Policy Series No. 71, Cape Town.

36. Piper, L. and Charman, A. (2016). "Xenophobia, Price Competition and Violence in the Spaza Sector in South Africa" *African Human Mobility Review* 2: 332-361.

37. Sibanda, O. and Sibanda. F. (2014). "'Land of Opportunity and Despair': Zimbabwean Migrants in Johannesburg" *Journal of Social Development in Africa* 29: 55.

38. Steinberg, J. (2012). "Security and Disappointment: Policing, Freedom and Xenophobia in South Africa" *British Journal of Criminology* 52: 345-360.

39. Tawodzera, G., Chikanda, A., Crush, J and Tengeh, R. (2015). *International Migrants and Refugees in Cape Town's Informal Economy.* SAMP Migration Policy Series No. 70, Cape Town.

40. Tevera, D. (2013). "African Migrants, Xenophobia and Urban Violence in Post-Apartheid South Africa" *Alternation* 7: 9-26.

41. Thebe, V. (2016). "'Two Steps Forward, One Step Back': Zimbabwean Migration and South Africa's Regularising Programme (the ZDP)" *Journal of International Migration and Integration* doi:10.1007/s12134-016-0495-8

MIGRATION POLICY SERIES

1   *Covert Operations: Clandestine Migration, Temporary Work and Immigration Policy in South Africa* (1997) ISBN 1-874864-51-9

2   *Riding the Tiger: Lesotho Miners and Permanent Residence in South Africa* (1997) ISBN 1-874864-52-7

3   *International Migration, Immigrant Entrepreneurs and South Africa's Small Enterprise Economy* (1997) ISBN 1-874864-62-4

4   *Silenced by Nation Building: African Immigrants and Language Policy in the New South Africa* (1998) ISBN 1-874864-64-0

5   *Left Out in the Cold? Housing and Immigration in the New South Africa* (1998) ISBN 1-874864-68-3

6   *Trading Places: Cross-Border Traders and the South African Informal Sector* (1998) ISBN 1-874864-71-3

7   *Challenging Xenophobia: Myth and Realities about Cross-Border Migration in Southern Africa* (1998) ISBN 1-874864-70-5

8   *Sons of Mozambique: Mozambican Miners and Post-Apartheid South Africa* (1998) ISBN 1-874864-78-0

9   *Women on the Move: Gender and Cross-Border Migration to South Africa* (1998) ISBN 1-874864-82-9

10 *Namibians on South Africa: Attitudes Towards Cross-Border Migration and Immigration Policy* (1998) ISBN 1-874864-84-5

11 *Building Skills: Cross-Border Migrants and the South African Construction Industry* (1999) ISBN 1-874864-84-5

12 *Immigration & Education: International Students at South African Universities and Technikons* (1999) ISBN 1-874864-89-6

13 *The Lives and Times of African Immigrants in Post-Apartheid South Africa* (1999) ISBN 1-874864-91-8

14 *Still Waiting for the Barbarians: South African Attitudes to Immigrants and Immigration* (1999) ISBN 1-874864-91-8

15 *Undermining Labour: Migrancy and Sub-Contracting in the South African Gold Mining Industry* (1999) ISBN 1-874864-91-8

16 *Borderline Farming: Foreign Migrants in South African Commercial Agriculture* (2000) ISBN 1-874864-97-7

17 *Writing Xenophobia: Immigration and the Press in Post-Apartheid South Africa* (2000) ISBN 1-919798-01-3

18 *Losing Our Minds: Skills Migration and the South African Brain Drain* (2000) ISBN 1-919798-03-x

19 *Botswana: Migration Perspectives and Prospects* (2000) ISBN 1-919798-04-8

20 *The Brain Gain: Skilled Migrants and Immigration Policy in Post-Apartheid South Africa* (2000) ISBN 1-919798-14-5

21 *Cross-Border Raiding and Community Conflict in the Lesotho-South African Border Zone* (2001) ISBN 1-919798-16-1

22 *Immigration, Xenophobia and Human Rights in South Africa* (2001) ISBN 1-919798-30-7

23 *Gender and the Brain Drain from South Africa* (2001) ISBN 1-919798-35-8

24 *Spaces of Vulnerability: Migration and HIV/AIDS in South Africa* (2002) ISBN 1-919798-38-2

25 *Zimbabweans Who Move: Perspectives on International Migration in Zimbabwe* (2002) ISBN 1-919798-40-4

26 *The Border Within: The Future of the Lesotho-South African International Boundary* (2002) ISBN 1-919798-41-2

27 *Mobile Namibia: Migration Trends and Attitudes* (2002) ISBN 1-919798-44-7

28 *Changing Attitudes to Immigration and Refugee Policy in Botswana* (2003) ISBN 1-919798-47-1

29 *The New Brain Drain from Zimbabwe* (2003) ISBN 1-919798-48-X

30 *Regionalizing Xenophobia? Citizen Attitudes to Immigration and Refugee Policy in Southern Africa* (2004) ISBN 1-919798-53-6

31 *Migration, Sexuality and HIV/AIDS in Rural South Africa* (2004) ISBN 1-919798-63-3

32 *Swaziland Moves: Perceptions and Patterns of Modern Migration* (2004) ISBN 1-919798-67-6

33 *HIV/AIDS and Children's Migration in Southern Africa* (2004) ISBN 1-919798-70-6

34 *Medical Leave: The Exodus of Health Professionals from Zimbabwe* (2005) ISBN 1-919798-74-9

35 *Degrees of Uncertainty: Students and the Brain Drain in Southern Africa* (2005) ISBN 1-919798-84-6

36 *Restless Minds: South African Students and the Brain Drain* (2005) ISBN 1-919798-82-X

37 *Understanding Press Coverage of Cross-Border Migration in Southern Africa since 2000* (2005) ISBN 1-919798-91-9

38 *Northern Gateway: Cross-Border Migration Between Namibia and Angola* (2005) ISBN 1-919798-92-7

39 *Early Departures: The Emigration Potential of Zimbabwean Students* (2005) ISBN 1-919798-99-4

40 *Migration and Domestic Workers: Worlds of Work, Health and Mobility in Johannesburg* (2005) ISBN 1-920118-02-0

41 *The Quality of Migration Services Delivery in South Africa* (2005) ISBN 1-920118-03-9

42 *States of Vulnerability: The Future Brain Drain of Talent to South Africa* (2006) ISBN 1-920118-07-1

43 *Migration and Development in Mozambique: Poverty, Inequality and Survival* (2006) ISBN 1-920118-10-1

44 *Migration, Remittances and Development in Southern Africa* (2006) ISBN 1-920118-15-2

45 *Medical Recruiting: The Case of South African Health Care Professionals* (2007) ISBN 1-920118-47-0

46 *Voices From the Margins: Migrant Women's Experiences in Southern Africa* (2007) ISBN 1-920118-50-0

47 *The Haemorrhage of Health Professionals From South Africa: Medical Opinions* (2007) ISBN 978-1-920118-63-1

48 *The Quality of Immigration and Citizenship Services in Namibia* (2008) ISBN 978-1-920118-67-9

49 *Gender, Migration and Remittances in Southern Africa* (2008) ISBN 978-1-920118-70-9

50 *The Perfect Storm: The Realities of Xenophobia in Contemporary South Africa* (2008) ISBN 978-1-920118-71-6

51 *Migrant Remittances and Household Survival in Zimbabwe* (2009) ISBN 978-1-920118-92-1

52 *Migration, Remittances and 'Development' in Lesotho* (2010) ISBN 978-1-920409-26-5

53 *Migration-Induced HIV and AIDS in Rural Mozambique and Swaziland* (2011) ISBN 978-1-920409-49-4

54 *Medical Xenophobia: Zimbabwean Access to Health Services in South Africa* (2011) ISBN 978-1-920409-63-0

55 *The Engagement of the Zimbabwean Medical Diaspora* (2011) ISBN 978-1-920409-64-7

56 *Right to the Classroom: Educational Barriers for Zimbabweans in South Africa* (2011) ISBN 978-1-920409-68-5

57 *Patients Without Borders: Medical Tourism and Medical Migration in Southern Africa* (2012) ISBN 978-1-920409-74-6

58 *The Disengagement of the South African Medical Diaspora* (2012) ISBN 978-1-920596-00-2

59 *The Third Wave: Mixed Migration from Zimbabwe to South Africa* (2012) ISBN 978-1-920596-01-9

60 *Linking Migration, Food Security and Development* (2012) ISBN 978-1-920596-02-6

61 *Unfriendly Neighbours: Contemporary Migration from Zimbabwe to Botswana* (2012) ISBN 978-1-920596-16-3

62 *Heading North: The Zimbabwean Diaspora in Canada* (2012) ISBN 978-1-920596-03-3

63 *Dystopia and Disengagement: Diaspora Attitudes Towards South Africa* (2012) ISBN 978-1-920596-04-0

64 *Soft Targets: Xenophobia, Public Violence and Changing Attitudes to Migrants in South Africa after May 2008* (2013) ISBN 978-1-920596-05-7

65 *Brain Drain and Regain: Migration Behaviour of South African Medical Professionals* (2014) ISBN 978-1-920596-07-1

66 *Xenophobic Violence in South Africa: Denialism, Minimalism, Realism* (2014) ISBN 978-1-920596-08-8

67 *Migrant Entrepreneurship Collective Violence and Xenophobia in South Africa* (2014) ISBN 978-1-920596-09-5

68 *Informal Migrant Entrepreneurship and Inclusive Growth in South Africa, Zimbabwe and Mozambique* (2015) ISBN 978-1-920596-10-1

69 *Calibrating Informal Cross-Border Trade in Southern Africa* (2015) ISBN 978-1-920596-13-2

70 *International Migrants and Refugees in Cape Town's Informal Economy* (2016) ISBN 978-1-920596-15-6

71 *International Migrants in Johannesburg's Informal Economy* (2016) ISBN 978-1-920596-18-7

72 *Food Remittances: Migration and Food Security in Africa* (2016) ISBN 978-1-920596-19-4

73 *Informal Entrepreneurship and Cross-Border Trade in Maputo, Mozambique* (2016) ISBN 978-1-920596-20-0

74 *Informal Entrepreneurship and Cross-Border Trade between Zimbabwe and South Africa* (2017) ISBN 978-1-920596-29-3

75 *Competition or Co-operation? South African and Migrant Entrepreneurs in Johannesburg* (2017) ISBN 978-1-920596-30-9

76 *Refugee Entrepreneurial Economies in Urban South Africa* (2017) ISBN 978-1-920596-35-4

This report examines the impact of xenophobic violence on Zimbabweans who are trying to make a living in the South African informal sector and finds that xenophobic violence has several key characteristics that put them at constant risk of losing their livelihoods and their lives. The businesses run by migrants and refugees in the informal sector are a major target of South Africa's extreme xenophobia. Attitudinal surveys clearly show that South Africans differentiate migrants by national origin and that Zimbabweans are amongst the most disliked. This report is based on a survey of informal sector enterprises in Cape Town and Johannesburg; and 50 in-depth interviews with Zimbabwean informal business owners in Cape Town, Johannesburg and Polokwane who had been affected by xenophobic violence. In many areas, community leaders are ineffective in dealing with the violence and, in some cases, they actively foment hostility and instigate attacks. The fact that migrant entrepreneurs provide goods, including food, at competitive prices and offer credit to consumers is clearly insufficient to protect them when violence erupts. However, the deep-rooted crisis in Zimbabwe makes return home a non-viable option and Zimbabweans instead adopt several self-protection strategies, none of which is ultimately an insurance against xenophobic attack. The findings in this report demonstrate that xenophobic violence fails in its two main aims: to drive migrant entrepreneurs out of business and to drive them out of the country.

BALSILLIE SCHOOL
OF INTERNATIONAL AFFAIRS

IMRC
International Migration
Research Centre

SAMP

UNIVERSITY of the
WESTERN CAPE

www.ingramcontent.com/pod-product-compliance
Lightning Source LLC
Chambersburg PA
CBHW080648270326
41928CB00017B/3232